1942: INTO THE BATTLE

29 USA

Allies land in North Africa November 1942

UNITED STATES POSTAL SERVICE

THE REAL STARS WERE IN THE AUDIENCE, AT HOME AND ABROAD

For most people in the United States, 1942 was a year of sacrifice. Moms and Dads said goodbye to their children with a hug and a kiss, a tear and a silent prayer. Youngsters wondered where Daddy was going and why he had to go there. Wives parted with husbands, and courageous young men put their lives on hold, postponed their ambitions, and volunteered for the war effort because they knew "Uncle Sam needed them."

The folks at home tightened their belts, too. They supported the military by working longer hours at the factories and cutting their spending so there'd be more available for those on the battlefields.

That was a year of change for me, too. I'd been packing my bags and travelling to places I couldn't spell ever since I first laced on a pair of tap shoes. This time, though, the places weren't on the Keith Circuit. This wasn't vaudeville, this was World War II, and our show wasn't the main act.

No sir, Freedom got top billing in this production. The people who sat in the audience were the ones fighting to protect our liberty. They were the real co-stars. Those of us who were on stage were supporting players. We were just trying to bring a little bit of home to these heroes—a package of laughter, songs and dances that showed these valiant men and women what kind of love and support was rooting for them and praying for them back home.

I logged a few miles doing military shows in 1942. Our troupe landed on grass runways, mud runways and a few

Enjoying the camaraderie of a handful of troops (left), Bob Hope regaled thousands of members of the armed forces with his comedy routines (opposite). The tireless entertainer was in the thick of hundreds of morale-boosting efforts during World War II and in several other conflicts for 50 years afterward.

runways that weren't even built until two or three weeks after we left. I got so many overseas shots that on a windy day I still whistle. But I met some of the greatest young men and women anyone could want to meet.

These kids were the strength of America, they were the courage of America. These were young men and women from all across our nation who all came to these foreign lands for one reason— because there was a job to do. Their homeland had to be protected, and they were the ones who would see that it was safe. They were willing to fight and sac-

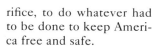

rifice, to do whatever had to be done to keep America free and safe.

Standing on the makeshift stage and looking out at those faces, I could see America. Our nation is many things. The song says it's "beautiful for spacious skies" and "amber waves of grain." It's blessed with many natural gifts from sea to shining sea. But our country's real power is, and always has been, her people.

Those were proud faces in our audiences. They were proud that America was founded on liberty and she was willing to fight to preserve it. They were

dedicated faces, people who were willing to make the sacrifices that freedom sometimes demands.

Those soldiers, sailors and Marines in our audiences were America's best. It's been 50 years now that I've been entertaining at military bases all over the world, and I'm still proud of each and every audience—in Korea, Vietnam and the Persian Gulf.

We all got applause at each one of those shows, and the ham in me would be lying if I didn't admit that I loved it. Yet I felt that I should be applauding them. They were the ones who were giving. They were the ones who deserved the applause, the gratitude. They were the heroes and heroines.

However, 1942 wasn't an easy year for any Americans—home or abroad. It was a threatening and a sad time. But it was also a time of dedication and renewed spirit. It was a year when all Americans resolved to do whatever they could to bring freedom and peace to the world. We all knew it would take time, but we were all up to the task.

It was that dedication that fueled Jimmy Doolittle's daring raid on Tokyo, our victories on the Coral Sea and in the Battle of Midway, our successes in Guadalcanal and North Africa. It was this commitment that gave us—all of us, in the factories, behind the desks, and on the front lines—the strength and the will to go on, and to assure our ultimate victory.

2

WAR TRANSFORMS ALMOST EVERYTHING

January 1942 found an America catapulted into the biggest war the world had ever seen, but an America with a mind-set that still clung to a slower, gentler past. Pearl Harbor had triggered a commitment to win that war, but without the realization that when peace came there would be no going back to the U.S.A. that was.

Washington, DC, was already changing as the new year began. Trains chugging into Union Station disgorged throngs. Suddenly the lobby's cathedral-high ceiling echoed a babel of arriving humanity that was competing for taxis, buses and directions.

To fill slots in an alphabet soup of wartime agencies—the WPB, OPA, OCD, OWI—some 5,000 new government workers were added to the payroll every month, and they brought families, who needed more and more consumer services, which soon couldn't cope. Housing and hotel rooms became items to fight over. Some beds had little chance to get made or even get cold; as many offices instituted round-the-clock operation, people who worked in shifts found they could also sleep in shifts.

A joke of the time involved a man desperate for a room who saw another man drowning in the Potomac River; instead of aiding the victim he demanded to know where he lived, then rushed there to rent the room, only to learn that he had been beaten by the man who had pushed the victim in. Newsman-commentator David Brinkley, who made an engrossing book out of all this, also told the story of a laundry so backed up that it stopped accepting new clients; it advised a young man clutching a wad of dirty shirts that his best bet for getting them washed was to mail them home.

Offices, desks, chairs, typewriters were scarce and coveted items in the wartime capital. There seemed to be a war among agencies to see which could get the most words on paper, and stenographers at times couldn't keep up with the increasing volume of dictation.

"As the forties began, Washington was ... a town and a government entirely unprepared to take on the global responsibilities suddenly thrust upon it," Brinkley noted. President Franklin D. Roosevelt had "to recruit an entirely new and temporary government, to be piled on top of the old one . . . to get the tanks and airplanes built, the uniforms made, the men and women assembled and trained and shipped abroad, and the battles fought and won ... A languid Southern town ... grew almost overnight into a crowded, harried, almost frantic metropolis struggling desperately to assume the mantle of global power."

Sixteen million Americans in uniform—that would be the ultimate total involved, and the training, equipping and fielding of such an unprecedented force transformed cities and much countryside. Last year's corn field was this year's airfield, and cattle ranges became firing ranges as the military took over huge tracts to teach war's deadly business. Wood frame barracks and corrugated metal Quonset huts proliferated in ordered ranks along the raw, treeless streets of vast new bases edged with warehouses, supply yards and motor pools and presided over by a bulbous water tower and a skinny flagpole.

Shipyards, aircraft plants and munitions factories sprang up and began burdening trucks and trains and cargo holds with the grim tools of combat. Arterial lines of supply uncoiled across the Atlantic to put troops and armor and planes in Northern Ireland, in Britain and in North Africa, and over the Pacific via a long chain of island bases to Australia.

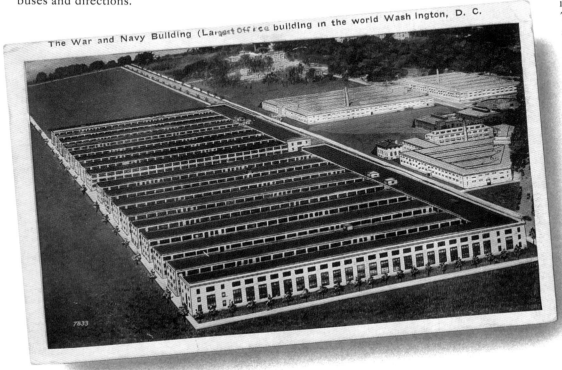

The War and Navy Building (Largest Office building in the world Washington, D. C.

7833

Greensward gives way to offices in wartime Washington. Called "tempos"—for temporary—some survived into the 1960s. War and Navy Building (left) was the world's largest until the Pentagon was occupied late in 1942.

Clerical army (right) competed for typewriters and desk space in the abysses of the War Production Board.

In early 1942, there were places those supply lines could not reach. Marines on Wake Island killed 700 Japanese in thwarting an amphibious invasion attempt, then surrendered to overwhelming enemy forces when no rescue fleet arrived. Americans in the Philippine Islands fought on despite growing awareness that vital arms and reinforcements could not come in time.

"Ships! Ships! All we need is ships!" That was a frustrated January diary entry by Dwight David Eisenhower. Before the year was out, he would wear the three stars of a lieutenant general and command Allied landings in North Africa. But as the year began, he was only a brigadier, a newly minted one at that, and he had been summoned from Fort Sam Houston in Texas to Washington by Gen. George Catlett Marshall, the Army chief of staff, and told to do what he could to get supplies and reinforcements to the sick and hungry defenders of Bataan.

But even if he'd had the cargo vessels he desired, the determined Eisenhower would also have needed planes to fly cover over them, carrier or land-based aircraft, and neither was available. The air and naval power he yearned for had been destroyed by Japan's initial hard-hitting strikes at Pearl Harbor and in the Philippines. He tried to bankroll privateers—small inter-island vessels—and even wangled a few submarine runs, but to no appreciable effect.

Americans at home, therefore, waited futilely for any good news from the entrapped U.S. troops and their Philippine comrades-in-arms. The drama of the foredoomed played out daily in press and radio. Inevitably it came down to a last message from the battered fortress of Corregidor, a requiem tapped out in staticky dots and dashes:

"They are not near yet. We are waiting for God only knows what . . . Damage terrible. Too much for guys to take. Enemy heavy cross-shelling and bombing. They have got us all around and from the skies . . . Everyone is bawling like a baby. They are piling dead and wounded in our tunnel. Arm's weak from pounding key . . . My name Irving Strobing . . . Sign my name and tell my mother how you heard from me."

Such tidings gave urgency to war efforts, but there was an uncomfortable irony in the fact that such bad times abroad seemed to beget good times at home. For an expanding body of defense workers, there were healthy paychecks, the fattest that many people had ever earned. As ever more plants opened, there were jobs, jobs, jobs. Suddenly came the realization that the unemployment problem had vanished, that the Great Depression, which had lingered through the '30s, had been vanquished into the history books.

With the heady freedom to home in on the best opportunities, Americans became a people on the move. Some went scouting to locate jobs and lodging before uprooting their families. Many simply loaded the family car, locked the house, and headed for Detroit or Galveston or wherever in America they heard jobs were going begging. A few went back but most never did. They came out of the hills and left the farms, and traded small towns for bigger towns, drawn by the good jobs.

Women left kitchens for assembly lines; blacks headed for cities, many in the North, as they found the way open to jobs previously denied. Here was the catalyst for social revolution that would still be at work half a century later.

The people caught up in all these changes remained largely unaware of them. They had a war to win, and they still had their ongoing lives to live.

June continued to be the big month for getting married, but in 1942 the furlough wedding, or even the weekend-pass wedding, was in. Brides still wore the traditional white, when they had time to buy a proper gown, but the trendy styles for grooms came in olive drab or navy blue. The immediate and prolonged separation that followed many nuptials put a great strain on marriages, and many were not equal to it. Part of the problem derived from peer pressure on women not to turn down a lovestruck serviceman. A song title of the day summed it up: "You Can't Say No to a Soldier."

The taste in popular music still ran strongly to sentimental lyrics, as in the 1930s. Many folks who were far from family for the first time consoled themselves with "I'll Be Home for Christmas." In a movie called *Holiday Inn*, Bing Crosby sang an Irving Berlin tune that everyone wanted to hear: "I'm dreaming of a White Christmas, Just like the ones I used to know. . . ." People nostalgically looked back to the way things used to be.

It was a popular theme of journalists that the troops were fighting for Mom and apple pie, and war workers were photographed scrawling dire promises to Hitler and Hirohito on new bombs and torpedoes. The war was being fought to resist the kind of changes imposed by the Third Reich on the Low Countries and Norway and Occupied France and most of eastern Europe and on the vast bulk of eastern Asia and the western Pacific that lay within Japan's "Greater East Asia Co-Prosperity Sphere." With victory won, GIs would return to a Main Street, U.S.A., that was still presided over by a town council and a state legislature and a Congress and President chosen in free elections, under the Constitution, so help us, God.

But the Constitution, surprisingly, came under an attack from within that was potentially more threatening than the attacks from without. Japan's devastating raid on Pearl Harbor had so shaken America's confidence in its defenses that enemy troop landings on the West Coast seemed possible. Hoping to sap the U.S. will to make war, the Japanese fed those fears with nuisance feints, shells lobbed at Fort Stevens, Oregon, by a submarine, incendiary bombs dropped on southern Oregon by a submarine-launched plane.

But rather than offer Japan a quick peace, the country reacted with a nasty backlash against the more-than 110,000 Japanese-Americans who lived near the war-jittery West Coast. In its way it was a more serious assault on cherished democratic institutions than all the totalitarian thrusts from without.

The threat surfaced in early 1942 as unadorned bias. Without offering any evidence of a security problem, the press and public officials began to militate for expelling Japanese-Americans from coastal states to the interior. "Herd 'em up, pack 'em off, and give 'em the inside room in the badlands," wrote a syndicated columnist. Others joined the outcry, which soon expressed itself in boycotts of Japanese-Americans: Grocers wouldn't sell them groceries, insurance companies canceled policies, banks froze their deposits.

Journey into limbo begins for Japanese-Americans (opposite), removed from West Coast states as security threats early in 1942. These evacuees sort belongings at Santa Anita racetrack, a "registration center." Tagged tots (right) await trains to desert detention camps. The Supreme Court freed detainees in late 1944.

Political pressure for sterner measures resulted in Executive Order 9066, signed by President Roosevelt on February 19. It gave persons of Japanese descent until March 27 to migrate voluntarily to inland states. After that they would have only 48 hours to sell their homes, furniture, farms and stores. In the sad dawn of March 30, they were driven to rendezvous areas, among them the Santa Anita racetrack, where some lived in horse stalls until 10 "registration centers" could be built.

Fearing that political stigma would attach to any appearance of leniency, state governors opposed giving haven to the exiles, so the centers had to be hidden away on remote federal tracts in desert country beyond the Sierra Nevada. There most of them would spend three years, guarded by sentries, barbed wire and searchlights.

The American Civil Liberties Union described their case as "the worst single wholesale violation of civil rights of American citizens in our history."

Unfortunately, that was not the contemporary view, and the issue did not reach a Supreme Court decision until December 1944. The court upheld the confinement as justified under the powers to wage war but ruled that the security threat had ended and the detainees should be released.

Strangely, the detainees displayed a patriotism for America that flourished under persecution and intrigued historian William Manchester: "To the confusion of their guards, they assembled each morning to raise the Stars and Stripes and salute it while their Boy Scout drum and bugle corps (every camp had one) played the national anthem." They formed classes to study the English language and American history, performed a variety of community services, and "on Saturday evenings they sang 'America the Beautiful'."

Their loyalties took convincing form after the Army, in January 1943, opened enlistment to Nisei (American-born Japanese). Swearing allegiance while still behind barbed wire, some 1,200 volunteered immediately, and thousands more ultimately signed up. Their fighting courage in the European theater was unsurpassed, and the 442nd Regimental Combat Team became the most decorated unit in U.S. military history. The regiment's members were awarded a Congressional Medal of Honor and some 52 Distinguished Service Crosses, 342 Silver Stars, 810 Bronze Stars and 3,000 Purple Hearts with 500 oak leaf clusters.

Most Japanese-Americans never got their homes and businesses back, and many who returned to their former communities in 1944 still encountered bias. In 1990, after many delays, the federal government officially apologized for the internment and began to pay the 60,000 survivors a reparation of $20,000 each.

Sadly, the totalitarian rulers of Germany and Japan made bias one of the deadlier weapons in World War II. Tokyo's militarists played on Japan's tradition of superiority over all other peoples. As late as the mid-19th century, barely four generations earlier, Japan had been a feudal society closed to the world for two centuries. "Stinking with foreign hair" was the language's term for outsiders, and any who ventured into the country risked death.

Commodore Matthew Perry shocked the Japanese out of their virtual cocoon in 1853 when he came calling at the head of a steam-driven flotilla. "Black ships," the people of the hermit nation termed his vessels, which defied the wind and billowed coal smoke, brandishing big guns fore and aft. Finding their shore batteries overmatched and embarrassingly outmoded, the Japanese bowed eventually to Perry's demands for U.S. trading privileges.

But the episode triggered a remarkable reversal of Japanese goals; in a few decades the nation would begin to demonstrate superiority not by isolation but by outdoing the "barbarians" at their own game. Such a goal explains subsequent Japanese history—the late 19th-century incursions into Taiwan, China and Korea; the destruction of Tsar Nicholas II's Far East fleet in the Russo-Japanese War of 1904; Japan's World War I acquisition of Germany's Pacific colonies; the scrapping of treaties that limited the size of Japan's fleet; the bids to conquer China and most of the western Pacific rim, which led to Pearl Harbor.

The samurai, a warrior class, had evolved in feudal Japan, initially to subdue the aboriginal Ainu. They became a force that perpetuated the prevailing order and infused society with sacrificial discipline. Their code equated defeat in battle with dishonor—and extolled death as a preferred option. One result was *seppuku*—a highly admired ritual suicide by disembowelment with a sharp blade.

A people inured to be hard on themselves not surprisingly could be even harder on their enemies who, after all, were considered barbarians. The 11,000 Americans and 65,000 Filipino allies who surrendered on Bataan on April 9 received a cruel lesson in harsh treatment. Most were herded on a forced march of some 60 miles, a journey under a tropic sun with never enough food, water, or medicine. To become too sick or weak to walk was a death sentence by bullet, bayonet, clubbing, being run over by truck, or buried alive. Perhaps 10,000 perished on the six-day trek which has entered history as the Bataan Death March.

Public-service themes replaced the hard sell as a savings bank issued a home-canning primer, ornamented with ration stamps and listing ways to save sugar. Tough weapons to match tough fighting men was the tack of Lockheed and Nash Kelvinator. Some battlewise GIs scoffed at the wild claims. But when they received adless U.S. periodicals, they complained. Reading the ads was like a letter from home.

Barbarism on a far grander scale was getting official sanction in Hitler's Europe in early 1942. At a January 20 meeting in Berlin, known as the Wannsee Conference, Nazi leaders planned the "final solution" of their problem concerning Jews in Germany and occupied nations. In simplest terms, they would be rounded up and shipped like livestock to concentration camps, where they would be herded in wholesale lots into gas chambers and crematoria for slaughter and "efficient" disposition of remains.

Actually the program had begun with arrests and confinement almost as soon as the Nazis solidified their political hold on Germany.

With war's outbreak it gained momentum. Now huge extermination camps would speed the genocidal process, which brought death to some six million Jewish men, women and children, plus untold others. The program was later known as the "Holocaust," from the Greek for a burnt offering consumed by sacrificial fire. Because Hitlerism held Jews to be *Untermenschen*—"subhumans"—who plotted to destroy the German master race, this absolute horror was held to be justified.

Americans in the spring of 1942 remained largely unaware of this horror, and the nation's Jewish community called for more coverage in the press.

Americans were also slow to learn details of the Bataan Death March, and they soon forgot about those Japanese-Americans hidden away in desolate detention camps. There was too much competition for headlines about the battles raging across the Soviet Union, North Africa and the southwest Pacific, about the Atlantic U-boat war that flared at times within sight of U.S. coast watchers, and about the crazy things happening in Washington. A bureaucrat, for example, persisted in getting the 11 endorsements needed to destroy some redundant files, and final approval was at last obtained— with the proviso that he first make one copy of everything destroyed.

One idea out of Washington that made sense was Claude Wickard's remark about home gardens. As Secretary of Agriculture, he was organizing all-out food production by the nation's farmers, but he noted that they had their hands full just feeding the Army and Navy and hungry Allies overseas. So there might be shortages of carrots and onions and potatoes and cabbage. And the problem could get worse because migrant workers were leaving the fields in big numbers to take defense jobs or enter the military, and the Japanese-Americans who had formerly grown much of the country's green produce were now in detention.

NATIONAL ARCHIVES WORLD WAR II EXHIBITION NOW TRAVELING THE COUNTRY

SAN ANTONIO San Antonio Museum of Art, San Antonio, TX 78215 (Dec. 7, 1991 – Apr. 5, 1992)
AUSTIN Lyndon B. Johnson Library, Austin, TX 78705 (Apr. 18, 1992 – Aug. 23, 1992)
ABILENE Dwight D. Eisenhower Library, Abilene, KS 67410 (Sept. 19, 1992 – Jan. 4, 1993)
WEST BRANCH Herbert Hoover Library, West Branch, IA 52358 (Jan. 30, 1993 – Apr. 11, 1993)
INDEPENDENCE Harry S Truman Library, Independence, MO 64050 (May 5, 1993 – Aug. 15, 1993)
GRAND RAPIDS Gerald R. Ford Museum, Grand Rapids, MI 49504 (Sept. 11, 1993 – Jan. 3, 1994)
ATLANTA Jimmy Carter Library, Atlanta, GA 30307 (Jan. 29, 1994 – May 1, 1994)
NEW YORK CITY IBM Gallery of Science and Art, New York City, NY 10022 (May 28, 1994 – Aug. 28, 1994)
BOSTON John F. Kennedy Library, Boston, MA 02125 (Sept. 24, 1994 – Jan. 2, 1995)
SIMI VALLEY Ronald W. Reagan Library, Simi Valley, CA 93065 (Jan. 28, 1995 – Apr. 9, 1995)
WASHINGTON, DC National Archives, Washington, DC 20408 (May 6, 1995 – Nov. 11, 1995)

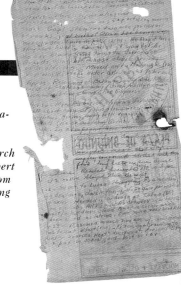

Diary written on cigarette paper during Bataan Death March by Col. Albert Svihra, from the traveling exhibition.

Enthusiasm for gardening took root, not only in backyards but front yards, downtown lots, park lands and even in vacant tracts within defense complexes. People who couldn't fight for victory found they could hoe for victory. By the fall of 1942, millions of Victory Gardens were providing 40 percent of the country's green produce. Some of the gardening newcomers thus acquired a lifelong hobby. Half a century after VJ-Day, a few patriotic plots in parks and on vacant lots still yielded annual bounties of early June peas and Kentucky Wonder beans.

There were many other options besides a spading fork for home-front patriots. Collection drives for scarce rubber, steel, aluminum and tin built junk mountains, sometimes in parks or right on the courthouse square, where they were photographed for posterity and the local press. Eager Boy Scouts filled church basements and empty storefronts with bales of old newspapers, helpful housewives saved cooking grease, and thoughtful tots collected aluminum pots and lead-rich toothpaste tubes. South Carolina Senator "Cotton Ed" Smith gave the rubber mat under his cuspidor, and Secretary of the Interior Harold Ickes offered his department's doormats. As comedian Jimmy Durante said, "Everybody wants to get in on da act!"

Certainly Hollywood was ready to get in on the act. Comedian Bob Hope, who was already visiting stateside training camps, discovered in the spring of 1942 that there were even greater GI audiences overseas. The discovery was made during wildly applauded visits to lonely military bases in mainland Alaska and the Aleutians; they were the first of hundreds of USO-sponsored tours that would take actors and entertainers to all parts of the globe.

The touring companies experienced hazards of wartime travel, heard air-raid sirens and bombs and ack-ack, visited hospital wards filled with maimed and wounded. Vocalist Frances Langford, a regular with the Hope troupe, recalls a bad time when she made an unfortunate choice of song. To cheer one GI patient, she began one of her standards, "Embraceable You," then realized with a start that he had lost both arms.

Not every touring company had a headliner like Hope or Bing Crosby or Jack Benny. But servicemen came anyway, crowding around improvised stages, sitting on sandbags, clambering atop tanks, filling hangars, shouting appreciation for being diverted from being so lonely and so far from home.

War bond rallies put Hollywood celebrities on stages that home folks could crowd around and get to see what James Cagney or Marlene Dietrich looked like in person. Exhorted by such extravaganzas, Americans bought $157 billion in bonds in three years, but the war was costing many billions more than that, and higher taxes became inevitable.

One tour cost the life of Carole Lombard, a leading actress and wife of matinee idol Clark Gable. After headlining a gala bond benefit in her native Indianapolis, in January 1942 she was killed in a Nevada air crash as she returned to Hollywood. She was honored as one who had given her life in the service of her country.

Following his wife's death, Gable joined the Army Air Forces and became an aerial gunner, among a host of stars who served in uniform. Jimmy Stewart piloted a Flying Fortress in bombing raids on Germany, Tyrone Power flew transport planes in the Pacific, and Robert Montgomery became a Navy PT-boat commander. Ronald Reagan joined a

U.S. Army film unit making historical and training features. Working with such a unit in 1943, director William Wyler documented the 25th and final mission over Nazi Europe of a B-17 named *Memphis Belle*, a piece of celluloid that would inspire his daughter to co-produce a feature-length film of the same name almost 50 years later.

The conflict was the theme for many of the 982 movies made in the war years. Released in 1942 were *Mrs. Miniver*, with Greer Garson and Walter Pidgeon; *Road to Morocco*, with Hope and Crosby and Dorothy Lamour, and *Casablanca*, with Humphrey Bogart matching wits with the Nazis in North Africa and Ingrid Bergman huskily asking a cafe pianist named Sam to play her favorite song, "As Time Goes By." It celebrated love's endurance in the face of separation.

In 1942, German scientists began testing V-1 buzz bombs and V-2 rockets; at Oak Ridge, Tennessee, and Los Alamos, New Mexico, sites were chosen for atom-bomb manufacture and research. Highest secrecy kept the world innocent of such terrors to come, and popular songs kept people's thoughts on humanity's kindlier aspects. Germans sang a ballad about a soldier's sweetheart named "Lili Marlene," and Americans really liked that number that Ingrid Bergman asked Sam to play: "It's still the same old story, A fight for love and glory, A case of do or die; The world will always welcome lovers. As time goes by." ■

Skies over the Pacific explode with the fury of the Battle of Midway, a decisive U.S. victory. Crippled by dive bombers, the U.S.S. Yorktown begins to list. Taken under tow, she was torpedoed two days later by a Japanese sub, and sank.

THE CHICAGO DAILY NEWS

Complete MARKETS

67TH YEAR—92.

SATURDAY, APRIL 18, 1942—THIRTY PAGES

SPORTS Final

FIVE CENTS

FIVE CENTS

U. S. FLIERS BOMB TOKYO

F.D.R. Names Board to Mobilize Men, Women

Kobe, Yokohama
Hit, Jap Report

FIRE AND PANIC!
JAPS SO SURE IT

FATHER JOINS SONS IN SERVICE

M'NUTT TO HEAD
BODY RULING USE

TOO BAD, EDGAR

DOOLITTLE'S B-25s BOMB TOKYO

The first astounding news came from Radio Tokyo itself: American twin-engined, land-based bombers had raided Japan's capital. But Tokyo was beyond the range of such planes. How could it happen?

President Roosevelt quipped that the planes came "from Shangri-la," a fictional utopia in the novel *Lost Horizon*.

The facts were truly stranger than fiction. A Navy task force had transported 16 Army Air Force bombers to within 800 miles of Japan. As huge seas rocked even the biggest ships, the medium bombers did what had never been done before. Heavy with fuel and bombs, they revved engines to near red-line, released brakes, and launched from the pitching deck of the U.S.S. *Hornet*.

This was to be a one-way trip. Too big to return to land on a carrier, the planes would raid Japan and fly on to fields in Nationalist-held China. Actually, the crews knew they would be lucky to reach those fields; they had to launch hours earlier than planned after the task force ran into Japanese picket boats.

First off, in less than 500 feet, was Lt. Col. James H. Doolittle, the mission commander, America's most famous flier. His aerobatics, instrument flying and speed/distance feats had won most major trophies. Each of the 79 men he led had volunteered for the high-risk mission.

Sixteen crews headed for Tokyo and other cities—Yokohama, Yokosuka, Kobe, Nagoya. Skimming rooftops to thwart enemy guns, the planes climbed only briefly so bombardiers could take aim. Black smoke and fire roiled in their wake as factories, docks and fuel tanks burned.

Darkness came on as the planes fled over the East China Sea, and the weather, which had turned sunny over Japan, became stormy again. In that dread night, 15 crews came down blindly in China, 4 by crash landings, 11 by bailing out. Parachute failure killed one flier, and two others died as their plane broke up upon landing.

Japanese invasion forces captured eight airmen. They executed three prisoners, convicting them under laws passed four months after the raid. Another P.O.W. died, but four survived three-and-a-half years of neglect, abuse and torture. One crew, too short on fuel to reach China, opted to land in Soviet territory and was interned for 13 months.

Following the raid, Japanese occupation troops in China killed an estimated 225,000 persons in areas where U.S. fliers had landed. Villages that aided the crews were obliterated.

As a military strike, the raid did minimal damage, but the psychological blow to Japan was enormous. The nation's antiaircraft chief took his own life. Forces needed on Japan's war fronts were tied down for home defense, and war strategies were changed.

For Americans the raid was a tremendous lift amid crushing defeats. Pearl Harbor had been answered by a tangible promise of total victory. ∎

Doers of the impossible, Jimmy Doolittle (second from right, opposite) and his crew pose with friends in China after leading a daring raid on Japan. B-25s (above) did the impossible by taking off from the U.S.S. Hornet. *Many lines secured the land-based bombers (left) to the carrier's pitching flight deck until takeoff. The planes hit Tokyo just as a practice air-raid alert ended, and some Japanese thought the bombers flying overhead were part of the drill. Some people even waved.*

Lessons in confusion, store shelves displayed ration-stamp point values as well as prices, a challenge for future homemakers (left). Pity the merchant (right), who had to post point values on the shelves, collect the stamps, and account for same. Shortages could develop without warning, causing panic buying and queues, such as motorists at gasoline stations (above). Despite problems, the rationing system succeeded because there was a will to make it work.

RATIONING HITS EVERY AMERICAN

The war taught Americans to do with less, even when they could afford to buy more. There was an ever-expanding military to arm and provision, there were Allies in urgent need, and the enemy at times held key sources of supply. There just wasn't enough of many items to go around.

The lesson in equitable sharing came in the form of rationing. With Japan ruling all Southeast Asia, including the Dutch East Indies, the U.S. lost its main source of raw rubber for tires. Tire wear could be slowed by conserving gasoline, which also faced increasing demand—so gasoline and tires were the first commodities rationed, beginning early in 1942.

Japan also held the Philippines, a principal producer of sugar, which was soon added to the list. Meat, most foods and shoes were included. And hundreds of items simply were no longer manufactured for the duration, including the annually restyled automobile.

The rationing process involved the issuance of rationing stamps, and the nation quickly became fluent in rationese, talking of A, B and X cards for gasoline, of red and blue coupons for food.

The war came home fast to American motorists. The military's appetite for fuels grew like Jack's beanstalk, and German U-boats patrolling the approaches to U.S. ports torpedoed many a wallowing tanker. Transportation difficulties resulted in a shortage so severe by the summer of '42 that many service stations, especially near the East Coast, posted "Closed/Out of Gas" signs. Drivers ran tanks dry, and even truckers were stranded. A tank truck might pick up a queue of a couple of hundred motorists, each hoping it was heading out to replenish a gas station.

The average motorist received an A card, generally good for three gallons a week. Business drivers carried B cards that had three levels of entitlement. Doctors, veterinarians and some public safety workers got X cards and unlimited gasoline allowances.

There was a special T card for commercial trucks and farm vehicles. Tractor fuel ran just as well in a car or pickup, a fact that could add popularity to the farmer's daughter.

Wartime Rationing imposed a monumental burden of issuing and accounting for stamps and coupons. The Office of Price Administration ran the whole system (which at times bogged down in snafus) and had to fight black marketeering.

The miracle was that the system functioned as well as it did. As it turned out, Americans ate better than they ever had, while at the same time feeding a record military machine and aiding Allies desperate for food and supplies. ∎

17

JAPAN HALTED IN THE CORAL SEA

After Pearl Harbor, Japan began to view the Pacific Ocean as its own pond. Its navy devastated enemy fleets in the Dutch East Indies and the Bay of Bengal. Armies blooded in the long China wars easily seized all Southeast Asia, including Burma, plus many Pacific islands. The major regional bar to complete Japanese dominance was Australia.

To deal with that problem, Vice Admiral Shigeyoshi Inouye assigned the Fourth Fleet to provide protection for troop landings at Port Moresby in Papua, New Guinea. From bases there, warplanes could neutralize Australia. Japan's navy could then control the Pacific from the Bering Sea to Antarctic waters. Australians were warned by Prime Minister John Curtin that "invasion is a menace capable of becoming an actuality at any hour."

That prospect caused Adm. Chester Nimitz, U.S. Commander in the Pacific, to dispatch a countering task force built around two of the nation's five surviving carriers. The arena for this first major sea battle of the Pacific war would be the 400,000-square-mile Coral Sea, bounded by New Guinea, the Solomon Islands, New Caledonia and Australia.

In the most intense fighting which ensued over this vast area, the surface ships of the two sides never sighted each other, a first in naval history.

Hundreds of American and Japanese airmen dueled each other and braved intense flak to attack and sink the surface craft of the enemy. Suddenly, the course of naval warfare had changed forever.

Vast distances and squallish weather hampered both sides in finding each other. After they did, the Americans sank the Japanese light carrier *Shoho* and heavily damaged the carrier *Shokaku*, plus taking a toll of planes and attendant vessels. The Allies also forced the enemy to abandon the island of Tulagi after a one-day occupation. The Japanese sank the carrier *Lexington*, damaged the *Yorktown*, and exacted a cost in other ships and in planes.

Both sides claimed victory but neither lingered for bows. The *Yorktown* headed for Pearl Harbor, quick repairs and a possible role in an anticipated battle somewhere around Midway. Japan's crippled *Shokaku* limped home for lengthy dry-docking, and although the *Zuikaku* survived, its use was limited by severe losses of planes and pilots. Japan's fleet fell back and the Port Moresby landings were tabled.

Thus the threat to Australia faded, never to regain believable dimensions. Japan would never quite cut the Pacific in half, and the Empire of the Rising Sun was virtually at zenith. That translated to a strategic victory for U.S.-British Commonwealth forces. Bitter lessons were also learned about the inferiority of some U.S. planes and arms, sparking remedial programs.

Both sides came away impressed by the willingness of the opponent to fight and die. ∎

A dive-bomber is signaled by a boatswain's mate preparatory to taking off on a run (opposite) in the Battle of the Coral Sea. American fliers sank one Japanese carrier and damaged a second in a critical engagement during which the surface vessels of the opposing fleets never sighted each other, a first in naval warfare. Japanese planes sank one U.S. carrier and damaged another.

Fires burn out of control (above) on the U.S.S. Lexington after hits by Japanese torpedo planes. Sailors calmly abandon ship, some enjoying ice cream carried in helmets.

Lifeboats (left) picked up all 2,735 who went over the side, but 216 died in combat or fighting flames. Standoff battle halted Japan's southward thrust toward Australia.

19

VALOR OVERCOME ON CORREGIDOR

For Americans who knew the war years, Corregidor is an emotional wrench. That island fortress at the mouth of Manila Bay fell May 6, 1942, in one of the nation's biggest defeats. Including the fighting on Bataan, the cost to U.S.-Philippine forces in dead, wounded and captured was some 90,000.

The Philippines' ordeal began three days before Christmas 1941. Some 43,000 Japanese troops landed from Lingayen Gulf and drove south toward Manila. Two days later, 7,000 Japanese seized Lamon Bay, southeast of Manila, and drove west. It was a pincers aimed at the capital, and Gen. Douglas MacArthur, supreme Philippines commander, declared it an "open city."

Following a long-standing plan, his forces fell back to Bataan, a mountainous, jungled peninsula between Manila Bay and the South China Sea. At its southern tip was the fortified island of Corregidor. The plan was to hold out until reinforcements came.

But in early 1942, the United States arsenal was short on ships, and Japan's land-based planes ruled the skies over the western Pacific. No reinforcements could get there in time. On paper MacArthur had 140,000 troops, but the vast majority of them were Filipino reservists, recently called up, short on training, arms and leadership.

His seasoned troops were a mixed bag of Philippine Scouts, Army regulars and National Guardsmen, plus a Marine regiment hastily pulled in from Shanghai.

On Christmas Eve 1941, MacArthur left for Corregidor. Ordered to Australia on March 12, he left Gen. Jonathan M. "Skinny" Wainwright to command a hopeless resistance. Except for a rare submarine or blockade runner, no relief ships got through. Lacking ammo, food and medicines, the defenders fought on, singing a derisive dirge:

"We're the Battling Bastards of Bataan; No mama, no papa, no Uncle Sam, No aunts, no uncles, no cousins, no nieces, No pills, no planes, no artillery pieces . . . ."

Bataan fighting ended April 9 with the capitulation of 76,000 sick, starving men, the largest surrender in U.S. military history. Wainwright's 11,000 men on Corregidor still fought on.

Pounded continuously by planes and artillery, the 3.5-by-1.5-mile island lost all semblance of a military post. Buildings, trees, lawns, roads and docks became rubble. Most defenders fell back into miles of tunnels in "The Rock," huddling among the sick and wounded. The dead piled up awaiting burial.

Even so, the bastion fought valiantly and slowed the first landings. But at last Gen. Wainwright surrendered to spare further loss of life. He noted that he did so "with broken heart and head bowed in sadness but not in shame."

Thus ended organized resistance in the Philippines, and Corregidor became another name to remember, with the Alamo and Pearl Harbor. In Australia, MacArthur was planning a return. ■

When General Wainwright (above at far left) yielded to General Homma (far right), Japan let this wirephoto reach the U.S. Hands raised, Corregidor's weary defenders (right) are herded by victorious Japanese.

In Malinta Tunnel (above), part of Corregidor's underground bastion, Army finance and signal corps units share cramped space and a hopeless vigil for help that would not come. After the surrender at Bataan, news headlines sometimes differed widely on numbers of prisoners taken, but there was consensus that they faced a grim and perhaps short future.

DAILY NEWS FINAL

36,853 FACE DEATH, PRISON AT BATAAN

JAPAN INVADES THE ALEUTIANS

Americans reacted with shock to the news in June 1942 that Japanese troops were in Alaska. Well, not mainland Alaska actually, but two islands of the Aleutian chain. Would Oregon be next?

Japan's bold reach into the New World was part of a grand strategy to kill America's will to fight. The scheme was put forward by Fleet Adm. Isoroku Yamamoto, architect of the Pearl Harbor attack, and it had two goals: (1) To provoke Adm. Chester Nimitz into dispatching a rescue fleet northward, weakening the forces protecting Midway, and (2) to secure the northern end of a far-flung ring of Pacific Ocean bases that would screen Japan's home islands from air attack. Nimitz refused to react to the Aleutians bait because he knew Midway to be Yamamoto's main target, thanks to U.S. deciphering of Japanese coded messages.

On June 3, aircraft from two Japanese carriers struck the first blow at Alaska, bombing Dutch Harbor on Unalaska Island. Army Air Forces P-40s based on nearby islands took a toll of the attackers, serving notice that the Alaska campaign might prove too ambitious. But a small U.S. naval force failed to make contact with the enemy, and Japanese troops landed unopposed on Attu and Kiska at the western end of the Aleutians.

A third contingent was to have seized Adak, but that move was abandoned following Japan's defeat at Midway.

American naval and air power soon turned the invaders into the besieged. Harassed by American planes when the world's worst weather permitted, despairing of resupply across vast ocean distances, the isolated Japanese garrisons found themselves futilely in command of "bog and fog."

In May 1943, the U.S. Seventh Infantry division stormed ashore on Attu and retook the island in a three-week campaign marked by prolonged, intense fighting. Finally boxed in at Chichagof Bay, the survivors of an original 2,400-man garrison expended themselves in fruitless banzai charges. At the end, GIs found themselves in charge of only 28 dazed prisoners.

A U.S.-Canadian force landed on Kiska in mid-August, only to find it abandoned. The Japanese forces had been withdrawn, some by submarine. Thereafter, the U.S. stations in the Aleutians would serve largely as launching sites for far-ranging patrols and repeated bombing raids on the Kuril Islands, north of Japan's home islands.

Duty in the Aleutians lacked the glamor of the war's main combat theaters. It often turned out to be months of monotony relieved only by letters from home or a rare USO show. But GIs serving there had the satisfaction of guarding the first U.S. soil recovered from the Japanese. After lapping tentatively at North America's offshore outposts for a year, expansionist Japan saw its fortunes ebb, never to threaten the continent again. ■

Sentry in the Aleutians guards a U.S. amphibious patrol bomber (opposite). Weather cost more lives than did the enemy. Patrols operated (left) in conditions so bad, crews boasted, that sea gulls hitched rides on the wings. Liberation troops land on Kiska (above) in August 1943, only to find Japanese invaders have fled.

23

U.S. BREAKS SECRET CODES

German and Japanese codes challenged Allied cryptologists. Nazis believed their Enigma machine (left) to be unbeatable. It used cylinders that could endlessly "reinvent" codes, but Allies deciphered many Enigma messages. Japanese machine used graduated wheels (above) to vary codes. Working with banks of tabulating machines (right), U.S. experts broke codes that revealed Japan's 1941 march toward war, and played a big role in America's victory at Midway.

In early 1942, radio waves over the Pacific crackled with orders to Japan's navy, transmitted in a seeming numerical gibberish. It was a secret code, of course—one using up to 45,000 five-digit numbers to stand for words and phrases. Unknown to Japan, the U.S. Navy had broken that code.

No sudden insight, the success had capped months of dogged effort by a small cell of cryptologists operating in a basement room at Pearl Harbor. The team, known as Hypo and led by Capt. Joseph J. Rochefort, was a part of the Navy's Intelligence arm. Japan was using the code, known to Hypo as JN25, to marshal a mighty task force for a showdown battle with the U.S. Navy.

History knows it as the Battle of Midway. With a 3-to-1 advantage in ships and planes, the Imperial Fleet should have won. But Japan lacked the weapon that had proved so effective at Pearl Harbor—surprise. Not only did the Americans expect attack, but they knew when and where. The cracking of the code was the difference. The U.S. won its biggest naval victory of the war. "Midway was essentially a victory of intelligence," said Adm. Chester Nimitz.

Codebreakers served the nation well even before the war began. In the fall of 1941, top U.S. officials were daily reading transcripts of messages in Japan's top diplomatic code, nicknamed PURPLE. A U.S. Army cryptographer, William Friedman, had built a machine, dubbed MAGIC, that duplicated the functions of Tokyo's PURPLE encoding-decoding machine.

As U.S.-Japanese relations worsened, Code PURPLE intercepts were like a right arm to Washington. Secretary of State Cordell Hull likened message contents to that of "a witness who is giving evidence against his own side of the case." As Hull waited on December 7 for Japan's tardy negotiators to deliver their terminal message, he already knew its ominous terms, thanks to MAGIC.

Unfortunately, MAGIC did not uncover the time and place of Japan's initial strike. Other intelligence pointed to the Philippines. Besides, there was an American prejudice that Hawaii was simply beyond Japan's reach. Hence, Pearl Harbor's battleship row and Hickam Field's clustered planes waited like pins in a bowling alley.

Codebreaking and electronic eavesdropping expanded astronomically during the war. Hundreds of codes were attacked with varying success. Allied listening posts also took radio bearings on enemy transmissions. By 1944 they could pinpoint Nazi subs in the Atlantic so fast that the once-formidable wolf packs scattered, fearing even to refuel.

On June 4, 1944, a specially trained Navy boarding party captured a battle-damaged U-boat off Africa's Cape Blanco, seizing the craft's codebook and cipher machine. From then on, the Allies sank U-boats at the rate of almost one a day. Electronic intelligence had made a decisive difference. ∎

Hard turn to port (above) saves Japanese carrier Hiryu as bombs dropped by B-17s churn the seas in the Battle of Midway. Later, dive-bombers like the Dauntlesses *(right) sank the Hiryu and three other enemy flattops which had taken part in the Pearl Harbor attack. Midway was a great victory as the above headline proclaims.*

U.S. WINS BIG AT MIDWAY

Until Lt. Comdr. Clarence Mc-Clusky's Dauntless dive-bombers arrived on the scene, Japan appeared to be winning the Battle of Midway. To that crucial point:

- U.S. bombers from Midway had bombed the approaching enemy fleet without scoring a hit.
- Japanese naval planes had blasted the key island base, preliminary to troop landings.
- Forty-one U.S. Devastator torpedo bombers had attacked Japan's carriers without a hit, and all but four were shot down.

But the ill-fated Devastators actually set the stage for the battle's pivotal events. As they skimmed the waves toward the Japanese task force, they drew flak and enemy fighter planes down to just above the sea.

That left McClusky and two squadrons of Dauntlesses almost unopposed as they roared down from high in the sky. They let their bombs fly at the Japanese flattops as the big carriers tried to recover planes returning from attacking Midway. Their hangar decks were a clutter of aircraft, fuel and explosives. Hits on the carriers *Akagi*, *Kaga* and *Soryu* set off chains of fiery blasts that proved fatal. In only a matter of minutes, Japan had lost three of its four carriers, and the tide of battle shifted to the United States.

By evening the remaining Japanese flattop, *Hiryu*, was sunk.

Entering the battle with three carriers, the U.S. lost *Yorktown*, which had been only partly repaired after damage in the Battle of the Coral Sea. Surviving and commanding the skies of the central Pacific were *Enterprise* and *Hornet*.

In command of those two carriers, Rear Adm. Raymond A. Spruance was a key player in the victory. When word came that enemy bombers were raiding Midway, he had decided to launch his own planes in time to attack Japanese flattops just as their returning aircraft attempted to land.

Although the Japanese still had a formidable surface fleet, without air cover they could only withdraw. Midway ended any effective threat by Tokyo to the Hawaiian Islands and alleviated invasion jitters along the U.S. West Coast.

Thus Adm. Yamamoto's bold design for defeating the U.S. fast and decisively, which he had begun so well at Pearl Harbor, came apart. He had to return home burdened by the first decisive naval defeat in Japanese history.

Adm. Chester Nimitz's decision to risk his Navy's only three carriers in the Pacific was vindicated at Midway, as was his judgment to form his battle plan around the information supplied by his code experts. The codebreakers enabled him to conceal his smaller task force northeast of Midway until just the right moment. The element of surprise, which Yamamoto had counted on so heavily, had swung to Nimitz, and the gameboard of the war in the Pacific now swung increasingly toward U.S. control.

But it was still a long way to Tokyo. ■

The heavy cruiser **Mikuma** *(left) smolders with fatal fires set off by American dive-bombers. Roiling smoke shrouds the Midway atoll's Sand Island (above) after Japanese bombers set oil tanks ablaze. Gooney birds remain calm.*

Women did it all in World War II, jumping into uniform or industry in record numbers, freeing men for combat. The Army, Navy, Marines and Coast Guard signed up some 400,000, and 19 million women eventually were part of the wartime work force, typing, filing, making all manner of weapons, operating huge cranes, repairing trains. Recruiting poster depicted smart martial attire; enthusiastic Texas shipyard workers struck a more casual note.

For your country's sake today—

For your own sake tomorrow

GO TO THE NEAREST RECRUITING STATION OF THE ARMED SERVICE OF YOUR CHOICE

WOMEN EXCEL IN WAR EFFORT

For an American high school girl in 1941, life's dream still turned principally on becoming a wife and mother. By 1945, her focus had widened enormously. The catalyst for change was a World War II experience that called women by the millions into a whole thesaurus of jobs and an estimated 400,000 into military service.

Typists led the advance. This conflict put more words on paper than any war before it; anyone who could type was needed pronto, mostly in Washington, DC. By bus and train women arrived, often going straight to a work-piled desk before finding a place to stay.

From keyboard beachheads, women took on varied jobs, but not as FBI fingerprint file clerks. The towering files, requiring ladders, were no place for a lady in a dress, J. Edgar Hoover said, and slacks were forbidden.

But slacks, coveralls, goggles and work gloves became familiar accessories of working women. There was Rosie the Riveter, there were welders and drillers, electricians and steamfitters. Women stenciled crates, stitched uniforms, packed medical supplies. They worked in locomotive shops and steel plants, in cramped stalls or drafty warehouses, at times with a spartan lack of amenities.

To free soldiers for combat, a Women's Army Auxiliary Corps was authorized in May 1942, headed by Texas publisher Oveta Culp Hobby. WAACs, later the WACs, took over GI typewriters and a lot more—trucks, supplies, message centers. The Navy, Marines and Coast Guard soon followed suit.

Despite doing the job, women often found slow acceptance. Work in heavy industry and the military carried a macho image that fought the romanticized notion of the girl next door. Wrote one soldier: "Why can't these gals just stay home and be their own sweet little self, instead of being patriotic?"

The frustration was particularly great for female aviators. Jacqueline Cochran, who had won the Harmon and Bendix trophies, had to fly a test hop across the Atlantic to win acceptance for women ferry pilots. The Women Airforce Service Pilots (WASPs) ferried combat planes, flew supplies, and towed aerial target sleeves for gunners. More than 70 were killed or injured in the line of duty.

High tribute marked deactivation of the WASPs in December 1944, but the women fliers had sought full Army Air Forces status, so they accepted the praise with mixed feelings. As the war wound down, men began to return to the work force, and many working women met resentment and job loss.

Still, the seeds of momentous change had been sown. U.S. women had done a great job and they knew it. In the words of one WAC, "I am doing something. I am helping. I shall continue doing all I can and be grateful for the chance. . . ." ∎

Rosie the Riveter gained fame from this Norman Rockwell illustration and a movie. The real Rosie was said to be Rosina B. Bonavita, who with a coworker drove 3,345 rivets in six hours.

Cleared for takeoff, Nancy Nesbit trains to get her wings as a WASP. Some 1,200 women graduated at Avenger Field in Texas and flew almost every type of military aircraft, chiefly as ferry pilots.

LINE IS DRAWN AT GUADALCANAL

Invincible was the word for the Japanese army in early 1942. Victory had rewarded every campaign in Southeast Asia and the western Pacific. Then came a battle for an obscure island called Guadalcanal.

Ninety miles long and 30 wide, this member of the British Solomons held palm-fringed beaches and lofty mountains, a tropical paradise. It also held fevered jungle, biting insects, swamps, big crocodiles, daily rains and quagmires underfoot. All this held only passing interest for the U.S. military until Japan decided in May 1942 to build an airstrip there.

From Guadalcanal, Japan's bombers could raid Fiji and New Caledonia, lifeline bases for supplying Australia. They could also attack Australia itself.

Admiral Nimitz decided that any airfield on Guadalcanal must fly U.S. colors. On August 7, Navy amphibious forces began to set Gen. Alexander Archer Vandegrift ashore with some 11,000 Marines on Guadalcanal and 6,000 on Tulagi. Before all supplies and reserve troops could be unloaded, the fleet protecting the landings was driven off by Japan's navy.

The Marines moved inland and seized a small perimeter encompassing the virtually complete Japanese airstrip (which they named Henderson Field for a Marine flier who crashed his plane into an enemy warship at Midway). Then, cut off from supplies and reinforcements, they became a bastion under siege. The enemy began a series of suicide attacks, many at night. The ordeal lasted until December, when the battle-dazed Marines were officially relieved by the Army.

Shouting "Banzai" and "U.S. Marine be dead tomorrow," the Japanese mounted a suicidal attack the night of August 7 on Tulagi. Dug in and with clear fields of fire, the Marines held and took a deadly toll. Tulagi fell to the U.S. the next day.

While battles raged ashore, six furious naval engagements were fought. Each side lost two dozen warships, but the U.S. Navy ultimately prevailed. Reinforcements gave the U.S. a winning hand. By February 1943, the last Japanese evacuated. They had lost 24,000 ashore and almost 4,400 at sea. More than 2,000 of their best airmen perished.

U.S. Marine losses were 1,042 dead and 2,894 wounded, the Army's, 550 dead and 1,289 wounded. Malaria and other diseases sickened thousands.

Other islands would hold horror for U.S. troops, but Guadalcanal proved they could endure the unendurable. For a grave in Guadalcanal's "Flanders Field," some gyrene had etched an epitaph on a mess kit with a bayonet: "And when he gets to Heaven, To St. Peter he will tell: 'One more Marine reporting, sir—I've served my time in Hell.'" ■

U.S. troops landing on Guadalcanal (above) set off six months of vicious fighting in a green hell. They withstood snipers and banzai attacks, at times accompanied by taunts: "Japanese boy drink American boy's blood." Diseases, crocodiles and stinging and biting insects thrived in tropical heat and daily rains. Whole camps became wading pools after veritable deluges (right), and it was an ordeal to keep guns and electronics operating. American forces prevailed over all obstacles.

AMERICANS LAND IN NORTH AFRICA

At last U.S. soldiers in numbers were on the move against Hitler. Americans awoke on November 8, 1942, to headlines that 34,000 had waded ashore at Casablanca in Morocco, 37,000 more had landed at Oran in Algeria, and 10,000 had joined 23,000 British troops at Algiers.

Operation Torch was under way, the war's first major Anglo-American campaign, with Lt. Gen. Dwight D. Eisenhower in command. Its goals included establishing control over French Northwest Africa, a worrisome unknown quantity since the fall of France. The move would also create a pincers on German Field Marshal Erwin Rommel's Afrika Korps, being pushed westward across Libya by British Gen. Bernard Montgomery's Eighth Army. It would answer Soviet Premier Josef Stalin's repeated pleas for another front. Finally, it might entice France's Mediterranean fleet into joining the Allies.

The campaign began to make household names of Eisenhower and other military leaders. The most colorful led the troops ashore at Casablanca. Maj. Gen. George S. Patton's ivory-handled revolvers, riding boots and blunt language conveyed memorable machismo. When an ammunition barge hung on a sand bar, for example, he waded into the surf and saltily instructed some GIs to join him.

They put their shoulders to the craft, on Patton's cue pushing it free to chug out for more ammo. He relentlessly drove his men, and the troops responded with a memorable nickname, calling him "Old Blood and Guts."

Another name marked for fame was that of Maj. Gen. Mark Clark. A gangling 6-foot-2 with chiseled face and hawk nose, he was Ike's deputy commander for Operation Torch. In an effort to prevent opposition to the North Africa landings by the forces of Vichy France, Eisenhower had sent Clark on a clandestine journey to Algiers a month earlier to negotiate with Vichy French officers. The scenario for Clark's mission was in the best *Casablanca* movie tradition: By British submarine from Gibraltar to a lonely Algerian beach; a furtive huddling over maps and notes with uniformed Frenchmen in a country house on a headland, interrupted by police; hiding under a trapdoor until escape could be made down to the beach, then almost drowning in the surf before regaining the sub.

Despite extensive efforts, Vichy French troops did oppose the landings. At Oran and Casablanca, the first casualties of the campaign ironically were shared by Americans, Britons and Frenchmen. French opposition soon collapsed, and French sailors scuttled their fleet at Toulon. Allied armies now could swing east to battle Germans, but the campaign had lost precious days.

In weeks ahead, green GIs would learn grim lessons in Africa through initial mistakes, welding themselves into combat-wise fighters, equal to the tests of Sicily and Italy to come. ∎

Desert warfare became the challenge after Americans landed in North Africa. The versatile Jeep, here carrying helmeted GIs (opposite), also could tow artillery, carry mounted machine guns, and transport wounded and supplies. Mobility was a key in the North Africa fighting.

Infantry on both sides faced barbed wire and mine fields (above) and devastating tank attacks (left).

U.S. forces in the combat theaters read war news in their own paper (lower left), published daily in European and Pacific editions.

33

AXIS FORCES GO FOR IT ALL—AND RUN OUT OF GAS

"Victory Disease" was how Japanese military leaders explained it, as they later looked back on the heady beginnings of 1942. Their most ambitious battle plans seemed to leap into reality, as if they held the pen of history and could write what they would on maps of Asia and the Pacific. Germany's war machine likewise had become a juggernaut that rolled on steel cleats wherever it would in Europe and North Africa.

But a specter of failure haunted the Axis partners, and it involved oil. Japan's warships and Nazi tanks devoured rivers of it, mostly from distant sources.

With the U.S. staggered by Pearl Harbor, the Japanese could make a grab for the oil fields of Borneo and Sumatra. But "Fortress Singapore" lay athwart their path, and the West pinned hopes on a considerable British Commonwealth garrison and powerful shore batteries awaiting them there. Japan's troops advanced down the Malay Peninsula, leapfrogged onto Singapore island's backside, and attacked the city. The bastion's huge guns could fire only out to sea—the wrong way! On February 15, Singapore's surrender shook Britain almost as much as Pearl Harbor shook America.

Singapore's demise left a potluck collection of U.S., British, Australian and Dutch remnant fleets to bar Japan from East Indies oil, tin, quinine and rubber. Under a courageous Dutch admiral whose orders had to be translated into English, the combined Allied force took on an immensely superior Japanese fleet. After seven hours of piecemeal battle on February 27, most Allied ships lay under the Java Sea. Japan had lost not a single warship.

Landings by two large invasion forces now proceeded, after being delayed only briefly, and Japan's conquest of one of the world's largest archipelagos, projected to take six months, was over in three. Meanwhile, an invasion of Burma proceeded apace. By late April, the Burma Road into China had been cut. The British surrendered Mandalay by May 2, and a U.S.-Chinese army led by Lt. Gen. "Vinegar Joe" Stilwell fell back into India to refit and retrain.

No wonder dreams of total victory gripped Japanese thinking like a disease! Just dispatch a force to seize Port Moresby and neutralize Australia, then take Midway and the Aleutians, in the process sinking the U.S. Navy's last-hope carrier force. Then the final curtain could fall on a triumphant Japan presiding at the peace table.

That's how Japan had it scripted, but the U.S. kept ad-libbing, and the first ad-lib was a shocker. On April 18, Jimmy Doolittle's bombers roared in from stage right and bombed the complacency out of Tokyo. And in early May, a numerically inferior U.S. carrier force fought a standoff in the Battle of the Coral Sea, causing Japan's Port Moresby invasion fleet to turn back.

The real surprise was that the Americans had read the script, thanks to brilliant U.S. codebreaking, and the finale was a decisive American victory.

Victory Disease also afflicted Germany's war leaders. Beginning in 1939, German arms had prevailed across Europe. To save Mussolini's routed troops in Libya, Rommel's Afrika Korps had driven British and ANZAC forces back to within 50 miles of Alexandria, Egypt.

Beyond lay the Suez Canal and a possible linkup with Axis partner Japan.

Germany's chain of successes owed much to Hitler's willingness to ignore conventional military wisdom. In 1942, his U-boats sank disastrous numbers of Allied ships, some near the U.S. East Coast, where Adm. Raeder concentrated submarine wolf packs. In early 1943, improved patrols, stronger convoys and codebreaking began to set the U-boats running for cover.

And even as Hitler foretold glories of his 1,000-year Reich, flaws in his genius were sowing defeat. Rating himself wiser than Napoleon, Hitler also invaded Russia. His response to stiffening defenses was to divide forces, hurling one fist at Caucasus oil fields while another hit Stalingrad. That city was taken at cruel cost, only to become a trap as resurgent Russians encircled it and lay siege. Hitler's zenith in Russia had been reached.

Likewise, the Germans in Egypt were never to take Suez. Near a village called El Alamein, British and Commonwealth troops on July 2 at last halted a weakened Rommel. In late October, Gen. Bernard Law Montgomery led a well-oiled British Eighth Army, reinforced with U.S. tanks, in the Second Battle of El Alamein. The Afrika Korps reeled back into a retreat that would become capitulation in 1943. Like Japan, the Nazis had overreacted to victory and reached too far. They were starting to run out of gas. ∎

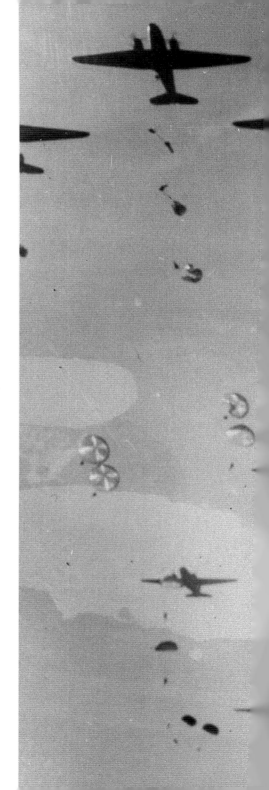

Paratroop jumps like the one at right gave war a new dimension. First U.S. use was Nov. 8, 1942, in the North African campaign.

OFF TO A ROUGH START, THINGS THEN GET BETTER

January 1 Declaration of the United Nations, a pledge to defeat the Axis, is signed by 26 nations in Washington.

January 2 Japanese occupy Manila.

January 7 President Franklin D. Roosevelt submits a record budget of $59 billion, $52 billion of it to fight the war.

Doolittle raid on Tokyo inspired this book, as well as others and a movie.

February 1 A daring hit-and-run American carrier force batters Japan's bases in the Gilbert and Marshall Islands.

February 1 Norway's Nazi-puppet regime renames Vidkun Quisling as premier. His collaboration with the Germans makes "quisling" synonymous with "traitor."

February 14 Japanese paratroopers land on Sumatra during their takeover of the oil-rich Dutch East Indies.

February 15 Singapore falls to Japan.

February 19 Japanese carrier planes bomb Darwin, Australia, virtually destroying the port and sinking eight ships, including the U.S.S. *Peary*.

February 20 FDR authorizes the internment of Japanese-Americans.

March 8 Japanese accept surrender of 100,000 Allied troops on Java.

March 28 Britain's Bomber Command stages a major night raid on Lubeck, Germany, leaving it in flames. Hitler calls for retaliation.

April 5 Japanese airmen bomb Colombo, Ceylon, off the southern end of the Indian subcontinent. They lose 30 planes but sink a British destroyer.

April 9 Defenders of Bataan surrender to Japanese after four months of fighting.

April 13 Byron Nelson defeats Ben Hogan and wins the Masters golf tournament.

April 16 King George VI recognizes Malta's resistance to a year of devastating air attacks by awarding the George Cross for valor to the island's "brave people."

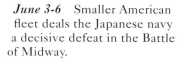

Junk jolts Japan in a "V"-for-victory poster.

April 18 Lt. Col. Jimmy Doolittle leads an air strike by 16 B-25 Mitchell bombers on Tokyo and other Japanese cities.

April 29 Invading Japanese in Burma reach Lashio and cut off the Burma Road, land supply route to China.

May 6 Gen. Wainwright and some 11,000 defenders of Corregidor surrender, ending organized U.S. resistance in the Philippines.

May 8 Battle of the Coral Sea is a standoff, but Japanese invasion fleet is forced to turn back from Port Moresby in Papua, New Guinea.

May 12 U-boat sinks a U.S. freighter at the mouth of the Mississippi River, killing 27.

May 15 FDR establishes the Women's Army Auxiliary Corps (WAACs).

May 30 British RAF sends 1,000 planes to Cologne, Germany, in saturation night attack.

June 3-6 Smaller American fleet deals the Japanese navy a decisive defeat in the Battle of Midway.

June 6 Japan seizes Kiska and Attu in the Aleutian Islands of Alaska.

June 17 Army begins publication of a weekly magazine for the troops called *Yank*.

June 21 Japanese sub shells the Oregon coast near Fort Stevens.

June 29 Italian dictator Benito Mussolini flies to Libya in anticipation of a Rommel victory in Egypt and the fall of Cairo.

July 4 U.S. bombers hit targets in the Netherlands, beginning the long aerial campaign against Nazi Europe.

July 4 Postal Service issues one of many war-theme stamps, a 3-center showing an eagle with wings forming a "V" for victory.

GIs voted pinup Betty Grable's legs "1-A."

We Can Do It!

Fisty female workers and famed crooner Frank Sinatra share America's heart.

July 10 Mussolini gives up hope of a victor's entry into Cairo, Egypt, and returns to Rome.

July 15 Gary Cooper and the legendary Babe Ruth open in *The Pride of the Yankees*, a film about Lou Gehrig's baseball career and fatal illness.

July 30 Congress establishes a women's naval reserve called the WAVES.

August 7 U.S. Marines make first amphibious landing of war, on Guadalcanal in the Solomons, beginning the long and bloody islands campaign in the Pacific.

August 9 British jail Gandhi after his drive to end Britain's rule of India turns violent.

August 25 The Duke of Kent dies in an air crash en route to Iceland, becoming the first member of the British royal family lost in the war.

September 21 Executions in Nazi Europe have risen to 207,373, the Inter-Allied Information Committee reports.

October 5 St. Louis Cardinals beat the New York Yankees in a five-game World Series.

November 5 Dead at 64: George M. Cohan, whose musical career was dramatized in a film, *Yankee Doodle Dandy*. His hit songs included "You're a Grand Old Flag" and "Over There," for which he was given a congressional medal in 1936.

November 7 U.S. and British forces land in Morocco and Algeria while the Afrika Korps flees westward from Egypt before the Eighth Army.

November 14 World War I ace Eddie Rickenbacker is found alive in a life raft three weeks after the bomber carrying him across the Pacific ran out of gas.

November 21 The 1,523-mile Alcan Highway across Canada to Alaska is officially opened.

November 25 Counterattacking Russians encircle Germans who are occupying Stalingrad.

November 28 Navy beats Army 14-0 before "hometown fans" in Annapolis.

November 29 U.S. adds coffee to the ration list.

December 1 U.S. gasoline rationing becomes nationwide.

December 2 Physicists at the University of Chicago create the first controlled nuclear fission, opening the door to the atomic age.

December 31 In a pivotal battle that helped secure the Arctic convoy route to Murmansk and Archangel, USSR, British destroyers in the Barents Sea turn back an attack on supply ships by a German battleship and heavy cruiser.

Love and intrigues of war brew a film classic.

During and after World War II, the U.S. Postal Service issued several stamps honoring people and places that played key roles in 1942 events.

U.S. AND ALLIES START HITTING BACK

A wonder of the modern world coalesced before the eyes of Washingtonians in 1942. Just across the Potomac from the Jefferson Memorial, the world's largest office building rose to five-story height within five-sided walls. The Pentagon, as it was inevitably known, would assemble under one 29-acre roof most of the burgeoning military command establishment, countering a helter-skelter dispersion of offices.

First occupied in November of '42, the gray monolith enclosed 3.7 million square feet of floor space and 17 miles of corridors across a former Arlington, Virginia, airfield. With such a vast area within a strange configuration, the Pentagon immediately entered anecdotal lore as the ultimate maze, architecturally and otherwise: A messenger boy was said to have gone in to deliver a telegram and three days later to have come out as a lieutenant colonel. To have been lost in the Pentagon became one of the badges of arrival in the wartime capital.

It also indexed the nation's swing to total war, a co-commitment with total mobilization of military and industrial clout. Its chasmal excavation was begun in 1941 while the country still wrestled the issue of involvement, and its concrete mass grew inexorably through the unifying catalyst of Pearl Harbor, the traumatic losses of Wake Island, Bataan and Corregidor and the crucial battles for Guadalcanal, Midway, the Aleutians and North Africa and for control of the shipping lanes of the North Atlantic.

With U-boat sinkings of merchantmen in American waters and Japanese air raids on Australian ports, the conflict by 1942 had touched six of the seven continents and arrayed 26 Allied nations—half the planet's population—against the Berlin-Rome-Tokyo Axis. Land masses suffering the greatest devastation were eastern Asia, ravaged by Japan's perennial China campaigns, and Europe, where the war had bled every major nation except neutrals Switzerland, Sweden, Spain and Portugal. The bloodiest fighting by far had swept across the western Soviet Union, and Hitler's flagging offensives still threatened Moscow and pressed a siege of Leningrad that would last into 1944.

A thousand miles from Leningrad, another siege held the world's attention in late 1942. Stalingrad, on the Volga River's west bank, controlled access to the Caucasus oil fields, and a major offensive to seize the city backfired in November 1942 when the attackers became the attacked. A Russian counterdrive encircled the Germans, by then in control of a metropolis reduced to rubble. Adolf Hitler forbade commanding Gen. Friedrich Paulus to break out or surrender, prolonging a terrible attrition into the next year.

Having lost 140,000 in the struggle, Paulus on February 2, 1943, capitulated with 91,000 sick and starving troops. All in all, Axis casualty figures, including Germans, Italians and Romanians, exceeded 1.5 million for the 1942 campaign alone.

Another debacle swept toward a climax in North Africa. In the face of resurgent Allied might, Germany's vaunted desert army hung onto a strand of Egyptian sand until the only recourse became retreat and defeat. That pro-

"Desert Fox" Erwin Rommel of Hitler's Afrika Corps (left) led troops that ran out of victories in the face of rising Allied might. WACs land in North Africa (right), the vanguard of thousands who served in faraway places.

cess also strung out into 1943, when 180,000 surviving veterans of the various Axis forces surrendered in Tunisia in May. But Rommel, named field marshal a few months earlier, had been recalled to help defend "Fortress Europe" and was not captured.

Thus, two major mistakes badly crippled Berlin's chances of ultimate victory. War historians have cited Hitler decisions that divided his forces too many ways, a parallel to Adm. Yamamoto's paring off part of his Midway fleet for a diversionary thrust at the Aleutians.

Top Allied commands meanwhile had laid down ambitious schedules for offensives in all major theaters. The Royal Air Force, building strength ever since its epic survival in the Battle of Britain, had begun in May 1942 to mount 1,000-plane raids on the German homeland. The continuing Battle of the North Atlantic, in which German subs tried to choke off supplies of arms and food to Britain, began to tilt in favor of the Allies. America's surging war production began to reach Britain and the Soviet Union in volume, and

U.S. forces grew inexorably toward an ability to fight wars on opposite sides of the globe simultaneously.

As the year ended, military thinking in both Germany and Japan had taken a conservative turn. On December 31, Japan would convene its first-ever major planning conference that was patently defensive. And the German general staff began to study where Allied landings on the continent might come and how to counter them.

Nazi and Japanese militarists had an image of a decadent America without the moral muscle to fight a long war. But the experience of 1942, from Bataan to North Africa, demonstrated a gross misreading of the national character: For good purpose, Americans had what it took for as long as it took.

Hollywood and the media depicted a fighting man driven to kill by hate of a barbarous enemy. But the average GI simply fought to get the war over with so that he and the world could be free to live a decent life.

There was another factor. "It's that sense of not wanting to fail your buddies," an ex-rifleman explained to historian Studs Terkel. The war was a lifetime bonding for those dependent upon each other for their very lives—and a camaraderie of all the men and women who worked in the cause, military or civilian, for the survival of the nation. ■

Imagine that you are an artist assigned to portray the Battle of Midway on a postage stamp. Also, the Battle of the Coral Sea, the assault on Guadalcanal, the landings in North Africa and six other significant World War II activities of 1942.

William H. Bond is the artist facing such an assignment, and before he completes it he will have set his brush to 50 such challenges. That's the total num-

ber of stamps he will design for the U.S. Postal Service's epic series on World War II, which is being issued annually in miniature sheets of 10 during the 50th-anniversary years of 1991 through 1995. The first 10 also appeared in the first of five special albums, published in 1991, and the 1992 set is seen in this album.

"Some themes are obvious," Bond says, "a carrier under attack, the Marines landing on a palm-fringed beach." But others offer no obvious image, and a usable idea may elude him for months.

"The most challenging so far has been the codebreakers," he says. "Cryptologists don't use easily recognized tools, and a lot of the codebreaking process is cerebral—even spiritual. How do you show that on a postage stamp?"

After considering several approaches, Bond depicted some World War II earphones and a pencil resting on a sheet covered with mysterious ciphers. The idea worked.

Such paraphernalia is not strange to Bond. London-born, he was a signalman in the Royal Navy in World War II. His main proficiency was with ship's blinkers and semaphore flags, but he could also don earphones and tap out Morse code.

Album text author Rowe Findley (left) and stamp designer Bill Bond relive a few of their World War II experiences.

Like Bond, writer Rowe Findley draws on memories of a personal journey through the hazards of World War II military service.

"Survival was uppermost in your mind," says the Missouri-born bombardier, "but later you remember things of no consequence—things that take you right back to a time and place."

So he set out to weave a sampling of trivia into the narrative of these albums—the movies people saw, the songs they sang and danced to.

"When you heard 'Don't Sit Under the Apple Tree (with anyone else but me),' it made a lot of difference whether you were hearing it in Nebraska or in the western Pacific, half a world away," Findley says.

He also mixes home-front incidents with those in combat theaters. His personal memory bank includes how good a Red Cross doughnut can taste in an overseas flightline canteen, and the redemptive qualities of plain old ketchup when applied to powdered eggs.

"Wherever you were, in uniform or not, there was a feeling of unity," he recalls, "We were in this together, all the way." ∎

Special thanks are extended to the following individuals for their contributions to the production of this book:

Eric Call
Print production procurement and supervision

Wendy Cortesi
Copy editing and research

Col. Charles A. Endress,
U.S. Army Reserve
Historical research

Rowe Findley
Narrative material

Bill Halstead
Editing and project management

Bob Hope
Introduction

Sharon Mann
Composition

Tom Mann
Design and layout

Fred Otnes
Cover artwork

Howard Paine
Creative direction

Susan Robb
Picture research

Jack Williams
Editing and project management

CREDITS: **Front endpaper**—Map of Manila Bay, Library of Congress. **2-3**—Bob Hope with sailor cap, National Archives; Bob Hope, courtesy Bob Hope Enterprises; Bob Hope entertaining troops, UPI/Bettmann. **4-5**—Excerpts from *Washington Goes to War*, by David Brinkley; War and Navy Building, private collection; Office workers, Martin Luther King Library, Washington, DC, from the collection of the Library of Congress. **6-7**—Lyrics from "White Christmas," words and music ©1940, 1942 by Irving Berlin, ©Copyright renewed, international copyright secured, all rights reserved, used by permission; Scout scrap drive, courtesy Virginia Historical Society, Richmond, VA; Woman Victory Gardener, Library of Congress; Package of fruit jar rings, private collection. **8-9**—Excerpts from *The Glory and the Dream*, by William Manchester; Japanese-American evacuees, The Bettmann Archive; Japanese-American children with baggage, Library of Congress. **10-11**—Fisher ad and Electro Metallurgical Company ad, ©*National Geographic* magazine; Texaco ad, ©*Life* magazine; Cohoes Savings Bank booklet, private collection; Lockheed ad and Nash Kelvinator ad, ©*National Geographic*. **12-13**—Lyrics from "As Time Goes By," words and music by Herman Hupfield, ©1931 Warner Bros., Inc. (renewed), all rights reserved, used by permission; Frances Langford story from the *American Movie Classics* original production, *Stars and Stripes: Hollywood and World War II*; Bataan Diary, Special Collections, United States Military Academy, West Point, NY; *Yorktown* hit, Library of Congress. **14-15**—Doolittle and his men, National Archives; Newspaper headline, Library of Congress; B-25 leaving carrier deck, National Archives; Bombers secured on flight deck, official U.S. Navy photograph. **16-17**—Child shopping, National Archives; Gas station car lines, Library of Congress; "A" and "T" ration stickers, courtesy Stan Cohen, Pictorial Histories Publishing Company, Inc.; Newspaper headline, Library of Congress; Grocer, Dmitri Kessel, *Life*, ©Time Warner Inc.; Ration coupon, tokens and stamps, private collection. **18-19**—

Plane cleared for takeoff, Smithsonian Institution; Newspaper headline, Library of Congress; Sailors abandon U.S.S. *Lexington*, National Archives; Lifeboat, National Archives. **20-21**—General Wainwright surrenders, UPI/Bettmann-Wide World Photo; Malinta Tunnel, National Archives; Newspaper headline, Library of Congress; Surrender, UPI/Bettmann-Wide World Photo. **22-23**—Snowstorm, Library of Congress; Kiska landing, Library of Congress; Plane on runway, National Archives. **24-25**—Nimitz and Hull quotations from *The Codebreakers, The Story of Secret Writing*, by David Kahn; Enigma code machine, ©Sam Tsunoda, U.S. Postal Service, courtesy U.S. Naval Security Station, Washington, DC; Japanese code device, National Archives; Tabulating machine room, Admiral Nimitz Museum, Fredericksburg, TX. **26-27**—Japanese carrier *Hiryu*, Smithsonian Institution; Newspaper headline, Library of Congress; Dauntless dive-bombers, Frank Scherschel, *Life*, ©Time Warner Inc.; Oil tanks burning, National Archives; Japanese heavy cruiser *Mikuma*, Library of Congress. **28-29**—WAC-related quotations from *This Fabulous Century, 1940-1950, The Patriotic Tide*, by Time-Life Books, quoting *A Book of Facts about the WAC*, Department of the Army, 1944; Recruiting poster, private collection; Shipyard workers, Library of Congress; Rosie the Riveter magazine cover artwork, printed by permission of the Norman Rockwell Family Trust, ©1943 the Rockwell Family Trust; Pilot in training, Peter Stackpole, *Life*, ©Time Warner Inc. **30-31**—U.S. troops land on Guadalcanal, The Bettmann Archive; Newspaper headline, Library of Congress; Veritable deluge, National Archives. **32-33**—GIs in jeep, National Archives; Soldiers break through barbed wire, National Archives; Tank, Eliot Elisofon, *Life*, ©Time Warner Inc.; Newspaper headline, courtesy David Eynon. **34-35**—Paratroop drop, U.S. Army. **36-37**—*Thirty Seconds Over Tokyo*, courtesy Ted Briscoe, photograph by Lauri Bridgeforth; Salvage sticker and Betty Grable, courtesy Stan Cohen, Pictorial Histories Publishing Company, Inc.; "We Can Do It!" poster, National Archives; Frank Sinatra, Brown Brothers; *Casablanca* poster, The Carson Collection; U.S. postage stamps, photograph by Lauri Bridgeforth. **38-39**—Excerpt from *The Good War*, by Studs Terkel; Field Marshal Rommel, National Archives; WACs land, UPI/Bettmann. **40**—Rowe Findley and Bill Bond, Pat McCabe, U.S. Postal Service; **Back endpaper**—Map of Oran, Algeria, Library of Congress.

HISTORICAL SOURCES: World War II produced a trove of historical volumes and materials. Especially useful in preparing this book were: *The Doolittle Raid* and *Doolittle's Tokyo Raiders*, both by Carroll V. Glines; *Corregidor, The Rock Force Assault*, by Lt. Gen. E. M. Flanagan, Jr.; *Blue Skies and Blood, The Battle of the Coral Sea* and *Japan's War, The Great Pacific Conflict*, both by Edwin P. Hoyt; *Miracle at Midway*, by Gordon W. Prange; *And I Was There,*" *Pearl Harbor and Midway, Breaking the Secrets*, by Rear Adm. Edwin T. Layton; *Delivered From Evil, the Saga of World War II*, by Robert Leckie; *Those Wonderful Women in Their Flying Machines, The Unknown Heroines of World War II*, by Sally Van Wagenen Keil; *World War II: America at War, 1941-45*, by Norman Polmar and Thomas B. Allen; *The American Heritage Picture History of World War II*, by C.L. Sulzberger; *The Two-Ocean War*, by Samuel Eliot Morison; *Chronicle of the 20th Century*, Clifton Daniel, editor-in-chief; *The Wall Chart of World War II*, introduction by John Keegan. Many other fascinating books and articles are available in your public library.

DATE DUE

MAY 0 5 2010		

GAYLORD   PRINTED IN U.S.A.

Front endpaper shows a map detail of Manila Bay with Corregidor and Bataan at lower left, the site of a major defeat during 1942.

The back endpaper map details Oran, Algeria, the site of a major landing during the North African campaign.

MEDITERRANEAN

(Jetty under Construction
for New Department Port)

W MERS-EL-KEBIR HARBOR

2900 meters of do
port has minimum

MONTE-CHRISTO

Fort Lamoune

Projection

Projection   23.7

Quarry   48.1

Bains-la-Reine
(The Queens Bath)   40.2   52.6

Navy Barracks   WM-9 meters

Post of Command   Battery   GUEYDON BASIN

Air Station

Cie Gle Transat.

NEW MILITARY ZONE UNDER NAVAL CONTROL   Central Wharf   PORT

(JUNE 1941)   165.4   Custom House   FIXED SIGNAL LIGHT (4M)

St Gregoire
Battery   WM-4.50 meters   Ste Marie   AUCOUR BASIN
Old Port   Wharf

244.7   352.6   Chapel of
Santa Cruz   Station Wharf

Ancient Fort Santa Cruz   DOCKS
Arsenal   Oran Naval Station

428.0   The Breach   134.7   Management

Pl.
Nemours   27.8

RUE CHARLES   RUE ST CHRISTOPHE

S' A. E. K. Morsli
(Marabout)   Pl
d'Orleans   Tribunal   New Chateau

Old St Louis Telescope   Pl de la
Republique   Casino
Military Hospital

Market   Pasha Mosque
Pl Kleber

BOIS   DES   PLANTEURS   Pl de
la Perle   Encampment   Police Hq

423.0   School   (Military Circle

The Terrace   113.8   Theatre   Fortress   70.5

379.2   KASBA   Hotel de Ville

Forest House   Campana Telescope   School

PLATEAU   162.5   Entrance of Ravin   84.8
Market

Cemetery   Laundry   Synagogue

ETIENNE   BOULEVARD DE L'INDUSTRIE   Law Cour

180.7   58.0   School   High
School

Powder Mill   Fort
St Andre